1·2·3 Draw
Mythical Creatures

A step-by-step guide

D1542424

by
Freddie Levin

Peel Productions, Inc

Before you begin, you will need:

- a pencil
- an eraser
- a pencil sharpener
- lots of paper (recycle and reuse!)
- colored pencils
- a folder for saving your work (portfolio)
- a good light
- a comfortable place to draw

Now let's begin!

Published by Peel Productions, Inc.
Printed in Hong Kong

Library of Congress Cataloging-in-Publication Data

Levin, Freddie.
    1-2-3 draw mythical creatures : a step-by-step guide / by Freddie Levin.
        p. cm.
Includes index.
Summary: Provides instructions for drawing a variety of creatures from myths
and legends around the world.
ISBN 0-939217-49-X (alk. paper)
1. Art and mythology--Juvenile literature. 2. Animals, Mythical, in art--Juvenile
literature. 3. Drawing--Technique--Juvenile literature. [1. Art and mythology. 2.
Animals, Mythical, in art. 3. Drawing--Technique.] I. Title: One-two-three draw
mythical creatures. II. Title. NC825.M9 L48 2003
743'.87--dc21

                                    2002156342

Contents

Important Drawing Tips:

1 Draw LIGHTLY at first, (sketch) so you can erase extra lines later.

2 Practice, practice, and practice some more, so you can get better and better!

3 Have fun drawing mythical creatures!

About Mythical Creatures

The word 'myth' comes from the Greek word 'mythos' and means story or legend. Myths were passed down from generation to generation as a way of explaining nature and the universe. The mythical creatures in this book come from many different places. Some are scary, some are beautiful, some are peculiar, but all are imaginary.

You can learn more about myths at your local or school library.

A Note to Parents and Teachers:

This book is designed to help the young artist break down complicated images into simple shapes and to see the relationships between the shapes.

To encourage young children, with little confidence or children with poorly developed motor control, cut circles, eggs, and ovals out of tag board. Have the child move these basic shapes into position on drawing paper and trace around the shapes, to get the first step of each drawing.

Once the first shapes are in place, the rest of the drawing can be added easily step by step.

HAVE FUN!

Drawing Basic Shapes

All the creatures in this book start with basic shapes.

 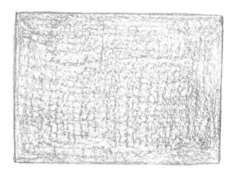 

Square   Rectangle

Circle   Oval (squashed circle)   Egg shape

Triangles   Trapezoid (triangle with one
                             point cut off)

Practice drawing these shapes, especially circles, eggs, and ovals. The more you practice, the easier it gets.

SKETCH, draw LIGHTLY at first. Then you will be able to easily erase your extra lines.

Adding Color

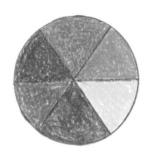

This color wheel shows the six basic colors. All the colors (except black, white and grey) are made from these six colors. Red, yellow and blue are called the PRIMARY colors. You can use red, yellow and blue to mix the SECONDARY colors.

Red + yellow = orange
Red + blue = purple
Blue + yellow = green

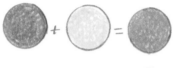

The final drawings, in this book, are made with colored pencils.
The colors used in each final drawing are shown in little circles, next to the finished drawing. Color your drawings any way you wish.

Add colors LIGHTLY at first. GRADUALLY add more color. Try BLENDING colors by using two colors that are neighbors on the color wheel.

EXPERIMENT to find your favorite combinations.

HAVE FUN with COLOR! Start adding color LIGHTLY! EXPERIMENT!

Sphinx (SFINKS)

The mysterious sphinx was a Greek and Egyptian legend. With the face of a woman, the body of a lion and the wings of an eagle, the sphinx liked to stop travelers and ask them a riddle. If they answered the riddle correctly, she let them go.

1 Sketch a small egg for the head, a large circle and a smaller circle for the body. Notice the position of each shape.

2 Draw curved lines for eyes. Add two curved neck lines. Draw two lines to connect the body circles.

3 Draw lines for the nose. Draw a long curved line to begin the front leg. Draw another curved line to begin the back leg.

4 Draw a curved line for the mouth. Draw a long curved line to begin the wing. Add curved lines to shape the feet.

5 Add more curved lines to finish the wing shape. Draw a long curved line for the other front leg. Add another curved line for the other back leg. Draw curved lines for the tail.

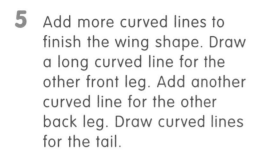

6 Draw curvy lines for the hair. Add a long curved line for the other wing. Draw short curved lines for wing feathers.

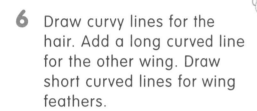

7 LOOK at the final drawing. Erase extra lines. Add color. Remember to start coloring LIGHTLY!

What riddle would you ask if you were a Sphinx?

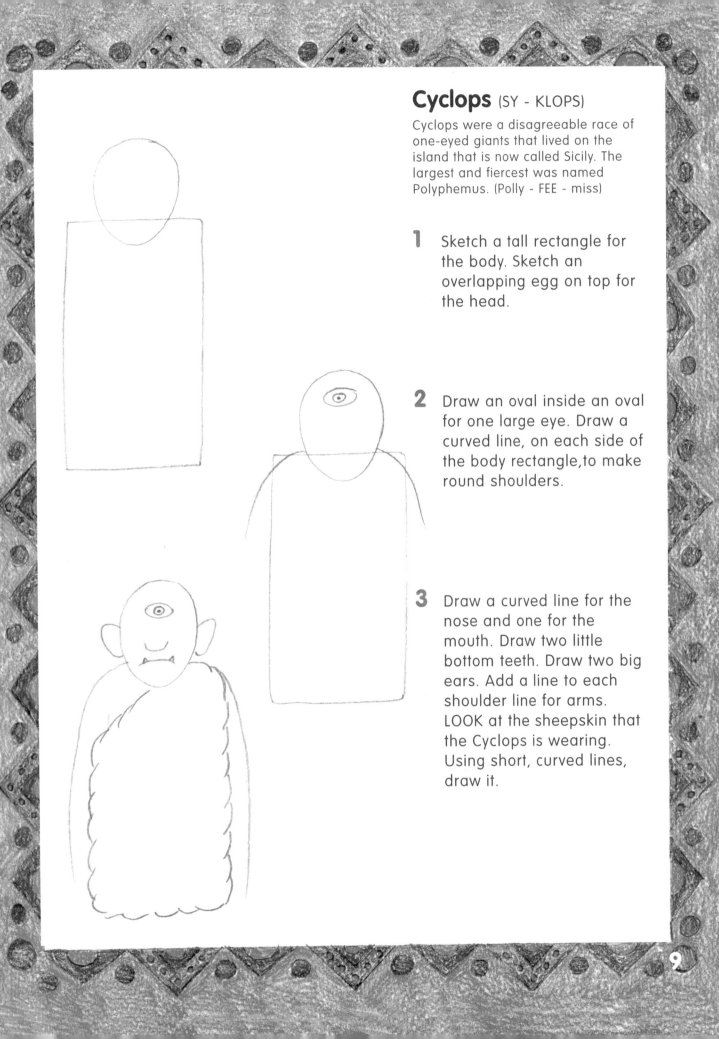

Cyclops (SY - KLOPS)

Cyclops were a disagreeable race of one-eyed giants that lived on the island that is now called Sicily. The largest and fiercest was named Polyphemus. (Polly - FEE - miss)

1 Sketch a tall rectangle for the body. Sketch an overlapping egg on top for the head.

2 Draw an oval inside an oval for one large eye. Draw a curved line, on each side of the body rectangle, to make round shoulders.

3 Draw a curved line for the nose and one for the mouth. Draw two little bottom teeth. Draw two big ears. Add a line to each shoulder line for arms. LOOK at the sheepskin that the Cyclops is wearing. Using short, curved lines, draw it.

4 Add a curved line to each arm line for the hands. Look at the legs and feet. Draw the shapes you see.

5 LOOK at the final drawing! Erase extra sketch lines. Darken the final lines. Add details and color.

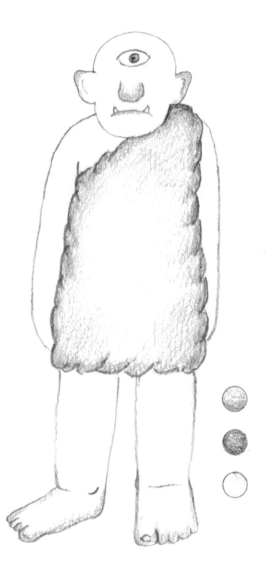

Pegasus (PEG - a - sis)

The story of Pegasus, a winged horse, is from Greek mythology. Pegasus was created by Neptune, the god of the sea and given as a gift to a young man named Bellerophon (bell - AIR-uh - fon) by the goddess, Athena.

1 Sketch a small circle for the head and a large oval for the body. Notice the position of the shapes.

2 Draw a curved line for the long shape of the horse's face. Add an eye, nostril, and a mouth. Draw two long curving neck lines to connect the head and body. Draw curved lines to begin one front leg and one back leg.

3 Draw curved lines for one ear. Look at the wing shape. Draw it. Using curved lines, draw the flowing tail. Using curved lines, add the lower part of the front and back legs. Draw curved lines to begin the other two legs.

4 Starting at the top, add the other ear. Draw curved lines for the mane. Add a second wing. Draw hooves on all four legs.

5 LOOK at the final drawing! Erase extra sketch lines. Add the details you see. Shade and color.

Perfect Pegasus!

Minotaur (MIN - uh - tore)

Half man, half bull, the Minotaur was a monster who lived in a maze called the Labyrinth (LAB - uh - rinth) on the island of Crete. Every year, young Greek people were sacrificed to him until, finally, he was tricked and killed by Theseus, son of the king.

1 Sketch a tall rectangle for the body. Sketch an overlapping circle on top for the head.

2 Draw curved lines for two ears. Draw curved lines for the bull's nose. Draw lines to begin the two arms.

3 Draw two curved horns. Draw curved lines for two eyes. Add lines for the bottoms of the arms.

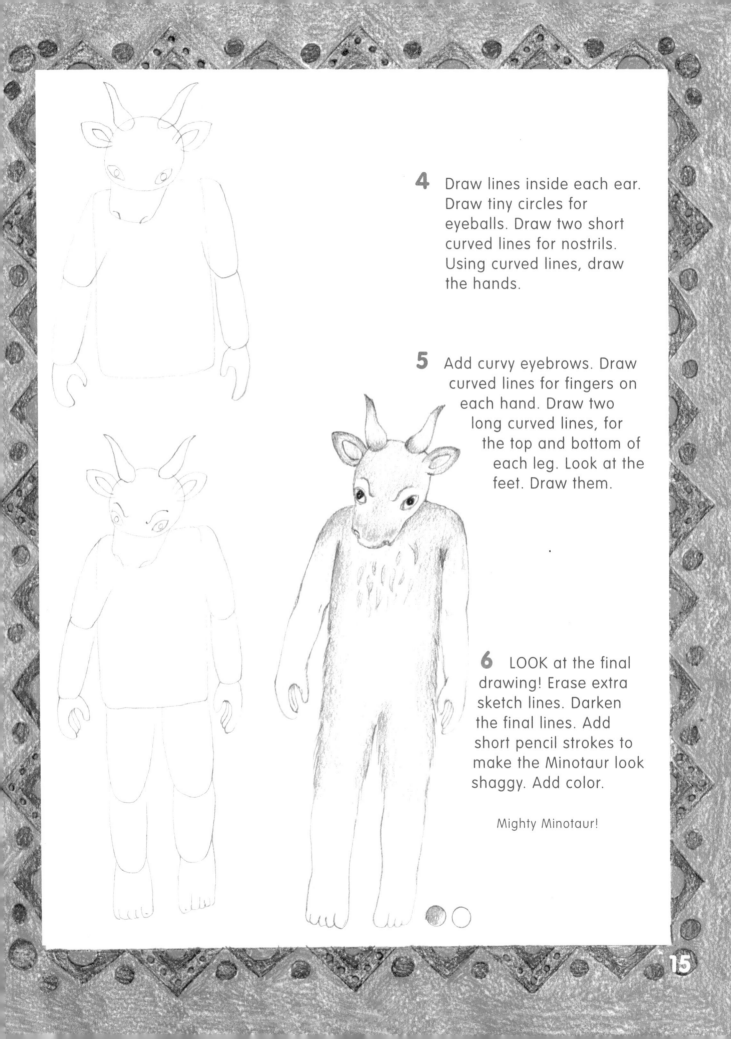

4 Draw lines inside each ear. Draw tiny circles for eyeballs. Draw two short curved lines for nostrils. Using curved lines, draw the hands.

5 Add curvy eyebrows. Draw curved lines for fingers on each hand. Draw two long curved lines, for the top and bottom of each leg. Look at the feet. Draw them.

6 LOOK at the final drawing! Erase extra sketch lines. Darken the final lines. Add short pencil strokes to make the Minotaur look shaggy. Add color.

Mighty Minotaur!

Cerberus (SIR - ber - us)

In Greek and Roman mythology, spirits and ghosts lived in an underground world called Hades. Pluto, the ruler of this world, created a fierce three-headed dog named Cerberus to guard the gates and make sure no living being entered Hades and no ghostly spirit got out.

1 Sketch three small circles for the three heads and two larger circles for the body. Notice the position of each circle.

2 Draw two curved lines to connect the two body circles. Next, draw two curved lines for the neck.

3 Draw two curved neck lines for the second head. Draw four curved lines to begin the four legs.

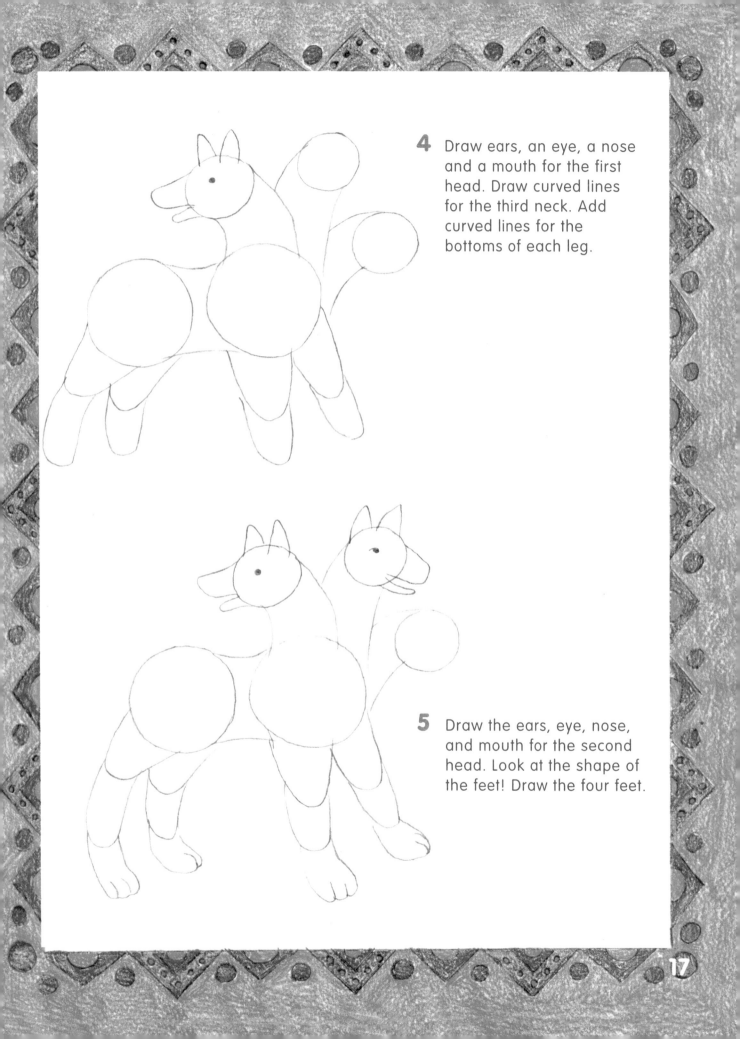

4 Draw ears, an eye, a nose and a mouth for the first head. Draw curved lines for the third neck. Add curved lines for the bottoms of each leg.

5 Draw the ears, eye, nose, and mouth for the second head. Look at the shape of the feet! Draw the four feet.

6 Draw the ears, eye, nose, and mouth for the third head.

7 Using a long curved line, draw the snake-like tail.

8 Draw curved lines inside each ear. Add eyebrows. Draw sharp teeth. Darken the nose tips. Draw an eye and a tongue on the snake-like tail.

9 LOOK at the final drawing! Erase extra sketch lines. Add details and color. Use short pencil strokes to make Cerberus look shaggy.

Scary Cerberus!

Centaur (SEN - tore)

The Centaur was usually a savage, wild beast, with the body of a horse and the head and shoulders of a person. A Centaur called Chiron (KY – ron) was the one exception, known for his goodness and wisdom. He can be seen in the constellation Sagittarius holding a bow and arrow.

1 Sketch an egg for the head. Sketch a rectangle for the upper body. Sketch two circles for the lower body. Notice the position of each shape.

2 Sketch two curved lines to begin the arms. Sketch two curved lines to connect the rectangle and the two circles.

3 Add curved lines to extend the arms. Draw a curved line along the side of the upper body. Draw curved lines to begin the four legs. Draw two curved lines to shape the tail.

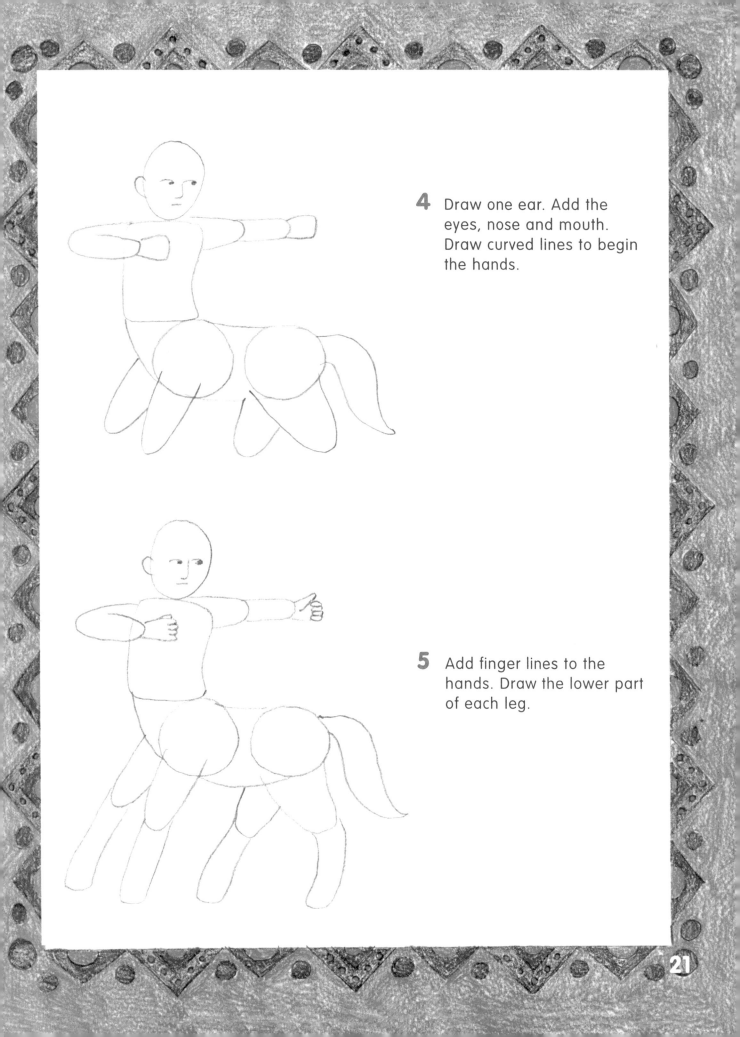

4 Draw one ear. Add the eyes, nose and mouth. Draw curved lines to begin the hands.

5 Add finger lines to the hands. Draw the lower part of each leg.

6 Draw curved lines for the hair. Look at the drawn bow. Draw it.

7 LOOK at the final drawing! Add the arrow. Erase extra lines. Shade and color.

Basilisk (BASS - uh - lisk)

A snake-like creature with the head of a rooster, the Basilisk could kill with a deadly glance of its fiery red eyes. The only defense against the Basilisk was to use a mirror to turn its gaze against itself.

1 Sketch three circles. Notice the position and size of each.

2 Draw curved lines to connect the three circles

3 Add a curving snake tail. Draw curved lines for the rooster's comb and beak. Draw an oval inside another smaller oval for the eye.

4 Look at the spear shape at the end of the tail. Draw it. Add a curved line to begin a front leg.

5 Draw a curved eyebrow to give a rooster's expression. Add a pointed tongue. Look at the wing shape. Draw it. Add a curved line for the bottom section of the first leg. Draw a curved line to begin the second leg.

6 Draw a nostril. Add lines to the wing. Draw curved lines to form the rooster's two feet.

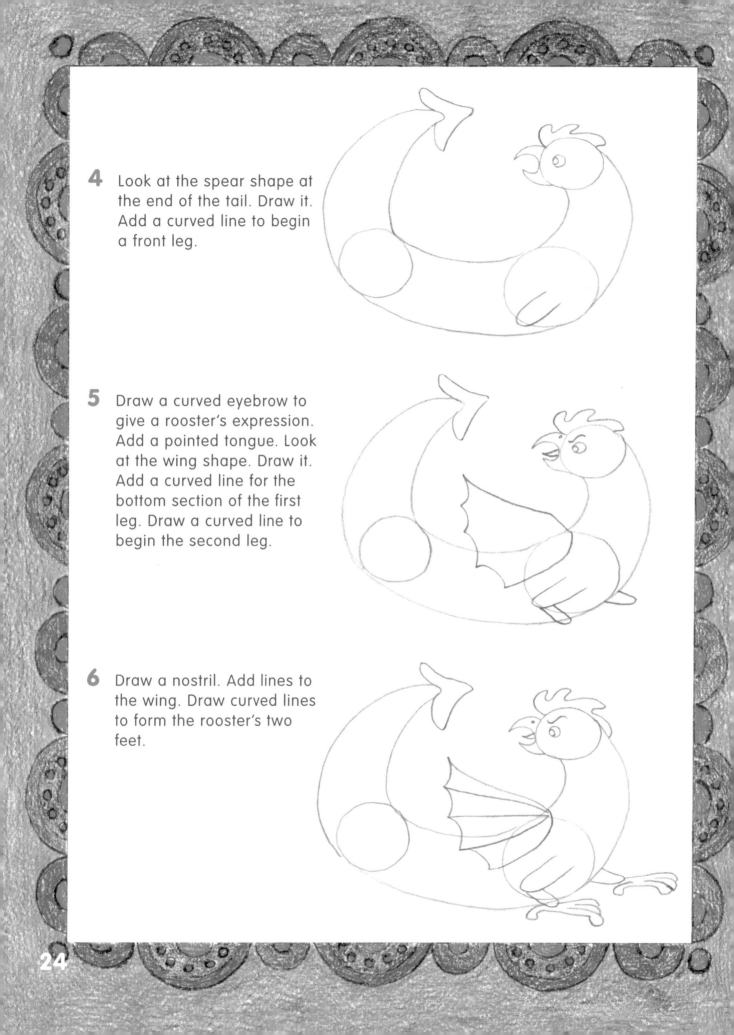

7 Draw short, curved lines for neck feathers. Draw scales on the Basilisk's reptile body. Add claws to the feet.

8 LOOK at the final drawing! Erase extra sketch lines. Shade and color.

Griffin (sometimes spelled 'gryphon')

A mythical creature from Asia, the Griffin had the body of a lion, the head and wings of an eagle and the ears of a horse. It lived high up in the mountains where it fiercely guarded its nest of gold and its eggs of jewels. Known for its great strength and courage, the Griffin became a symbol of power and bravery.

1   Sketch a small oval for the head and a large oval for the body. Notice the position of each shape.

2   Draw curving neck lines to connect the head and body. Add an eye. Draw curved lines to shape the beak. Add a curving tail.

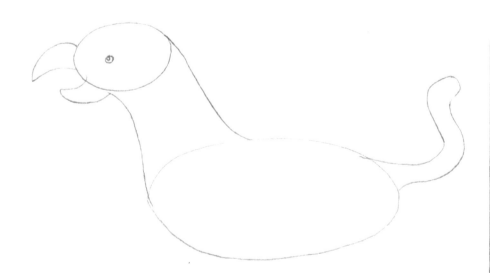

3 Look at the shape of the wing. Draw it. Draw jagged lines to make the clump of hair on the end of the tail. Look at the front and back legs. Draw the shapes you see to begin the legs.

4 Draw two eagle feet on the front legs. Draw two lion paws on the back legs. Draw a curved line to shape the belly of the Griffin.

5 Draw two ears. Draw a curved eyebrow. Notice how this changes the expression. Add a tongue. Draw jagged feathers on the neck. Add curved lines for feathers on the wing. Draw claws on all four feet.

6 LOOK at the final drawing! Erase extra sketch lines. Shade and color.

GREAT Griffin!

Hippogriff (HIP - po - griff)

In Medieval Italian poetry, the Hippogriff was a symbol for love. Born from an egg, it was a cross between a Griffin and a horse. The Hippogriff lived in the mountains where it could run like a horse and fly like an eagle.

1 Sketch a small oval for the head and a large oval for the body.

2 Draw an eye and a beak. Add two curved neck lines. Draw curved and jagged lines to begin the front leg. Draw a curved line to begin the back leg.

3 Draw two curved lines for the ear. Draw jagged neck feathers. LOOK at the wing shape. Draw it. Add the lower section of the back leg. Draw a curved line to begin the other back leg. Draw curved and jagged lines to begin the other front leg. Add a foot to the front leg.

4 Draw the other ear. Draw a curved line for the second wing. Add curved lines for neck and wing feathers. Draw the long flowing tail. Draw the bottom section of the other leg. Draw a line on each leg for hooves. Draw the second front foot. Add claws.

5 LOOK at the final drawing! Erase extra sketch lines. Shade and color. Put your Hippogriff on top of a mountain.

Would you like to ride on a Hippogriff?

Unicorn (YOU - nee - KORN)

The most magical of beasts was the unicorn, believed to have the power to cure all illness. A white horse with a single horn on its forehead, the unicorn could not be captured except by a beautiful maiden. Many thought the tusk of a narwhal, a real sea-going mammal, was a unicorn's horn. (See a drawing of a narwhal on page 32.)

1 Sketch a circle for the head and an oval for the body.

2 Draw a curved line for the unicorn's nose. Draw two curved lines for the neck. Look at the position of the legs. Draw four curved lines to begin the legs.

3 Add an ear. Draw the eye and nostril. Draw two curved lines to begin the tail. Draw the lower part of each leg.

4 Starting at the top, draw a small curved line for the inner ear. Add the long, pointed horn. Draw squiggly lines for the mane. Draw a curved line for the Unicorn's back. Add curved lines to finish the tail. Draw hooves on all four legs.

5 LOOK at the final drawing! Erase extra sketch lines. Draw the details you see. Shade and color.

Cute Unicorn!

Mermaid

Half human and half fish, the mermaid is a female water spirit. Tales about these beautiful, mysterious creatures singing haunting songs and warning sailors about approaching storms come from many different places. Mermaids are often pictured sitting near the sea on rocks, looking into a mirror and combing their long hair.

1 First, look closely at the position of the four shapes. Sketch a circle for the head. a gently rounded trapezoid for the upper body and a large circle and a smaller circle for the lower body.

2 Draw two curving neck lines. Draw two long curving lines to begin the arms.

3 Draw a curved line for the lower part of both arms. Draw two long curved lines to connect the trapezoid and the two circles. Look at the mermaid's fish tale. Draw it.

4 Starting at the top, draw long flowing hair lines. Look at the shape of her hands. Draw these.

5 Look at the shape of the mirror. Draw it. Add finger lines on both hands.

6 LOOK at the final drawing! Erase extra sketch lines. Add the details you see. Shade and color. Don't forget the clipper ship sailing by!

European dragon

In Europe, during the Middle Ages, people believed dragons were huge, terrifying winged reptiles that breathed fire, loved gold and jewels, and ate beautiful maidens. Stories were told about brave knights in armor who battled dragons to rescue the maidens, and capture the treasure that the dragon guarded so fiercely.

1 Sketch a small oval for the head and a larger oval for the body. Notice the way each oval is tilted.

2 Draw an ear. Look at the shape of the dragon's snout and jaw. Draw it. Draw two curving neck lines, connecting the head and body.

3 Add another ear. Draw an eye and a nostril. Draw a long curving line to begin a wing. Draw four short curved lines to begin the front and back legs.

4 Draw a line for the inner ear. Look carefully at the wing shape. Add two more curved wing lines. Draw the lower part of the four legs.

5 Add a long curved line to the wing top. Look at the shape of each hand. Draw the hands. Look at the shape of the feet. Draw the feet.

6 Add more curved lines to finish the wing shape. Draw the long curving tail.

7 Starting at the top, draw the second wing. Add straight lines to the first wing. Look at the fire coming out of the dragon's mouth. Draw it. Draw curved lines along his neck and belly. Add claws to the feet. Draw the tip of the tail.

8 LOOK at the final drawing! Erase extra sketch lines. Add details you see. Shade and color.

Dynamite Dragon!

Chinese dragon

In China, dragons were seen as kind and helpful and a sign of good fortune. When they were happy, they made a gong sound, and when they were sad, they wept pearls. Dragon designs were a favorite theme for flags, clothing, furniture, and art work.

1 To start your Chinese dragon, sketch four circles. Notice the position of the circles.

2 Look at the shape of the dragon. Draw two long curving lines to connect the circles and begin the tail.

3 Draw curved lines to make the snout and jaw. Draw four curved lines to begin the four legs. Add spikes to the tail.

4 Starting at the top, draw two circles for the nostrils and the eyes. Add jagged lines for spikes on the dragon's head. Draw curved lines for the lower part of each leg.

5 Look at all the spikes. Draw the spiky beard on the nose and chin. Add spiky eyebrows. Draw spikes all along its back. Draw four feet with sharp claws.

6 LOOK at the final drawing! Erase extra sketch lines. Add the details you see. Shade and color.

Kappa

A Japanese river demon, the Kappa has the body of a tortoise, the legs and feet of a frog and the head of a monkey. If you are polite and bow low when you greet it, the Kappa will bow low back and all of its strength will spill out of an opening at the top of its head. Then, you can run away!

1 Sketch a small circle for the head and a larger circle for the body. Notice how they are touching.

2 Using curved lines, draw the shape of the tortoise shell around the body circle.

3 Draw the round opening at the top of the Kappa's head. Draw the eyes, nose, mouth and ear.

4 Look at the Kappa's two front legs and feet. Draw these.

5 Look at the back legs and feet. Draw these. Erase extra sketch lines.

6 Look at the pattern on the tortoise shell. Using curved lines, draw the pattern. Draw a long curved line under the shell for the Kappa's belly.

7 LOOK at the final drawing! Add the details you see. Shade and color.

Cool Kappa!

Phoenix (FEE - nix)

A symbol of hope and renewal, the Phoenix was the mythical sun bird of Arabia who lived in a land of springtime with no sadness. Every five hundred years, the Phoenix burst into flames and died. A new Phoenix was born from the ashes of the fire.

1 Sketch a small circle for its head and an oval for the body. Notice the position of the two shapes.

2 Using curved lines, draw the beak. Add an eye. Draw two curved neck lines. Draw four curved lines to begin the two legs.

3 Look at the tail feathers. Draw these. Draw four curved lines for the lower part of the legs.

4 Look at the shape of the wings. Draw the wings. Add curved lines to form the feet.

5 Look at the feathers on the head crest. Draw these. Add curved lines for feathers on the wings. Add claws to the feet.

6 LOOK at the final drawing. Add the details you see. Erase extra sketch lines. Shade and color.

Fabulous Phoenix!

Genie (JEE - nee)

From Arabian fairy tales, the genie was a mystical and powerful helper. Created from flames and made of air and fire, the genie grants wishes. Controlled by its master, usually the owner of a special object such as Aladdin's Lamp, a genie can be good or bad.

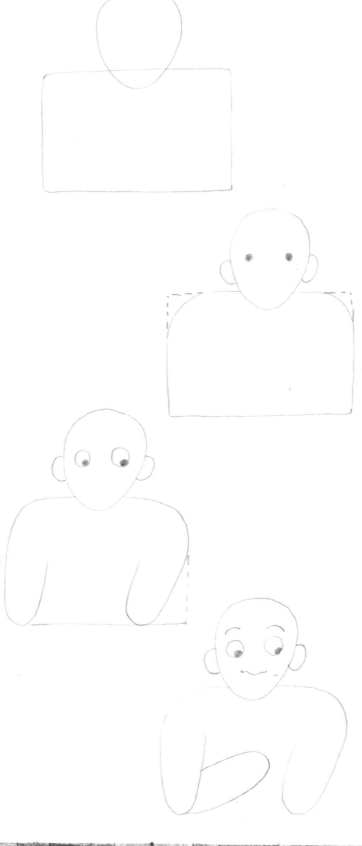

1 Sketch a rectangle for the upper body and an overlapping egg for the head.

2 Draw two dark circles to begin the eyes. Draw two curved lines for ears. Draw a curved line on each side of the rectangle, to make round shoulders and erase the sketch lines.

3 Draw circles around the dark eye circles. Notice how that changes the Genie's expression. Draw curved lines to begin the arms. Erase the sketch lines of the rectangle.

4 Add curved eyebrows and a nose. Draw a curved line to make the lower part of one arm.

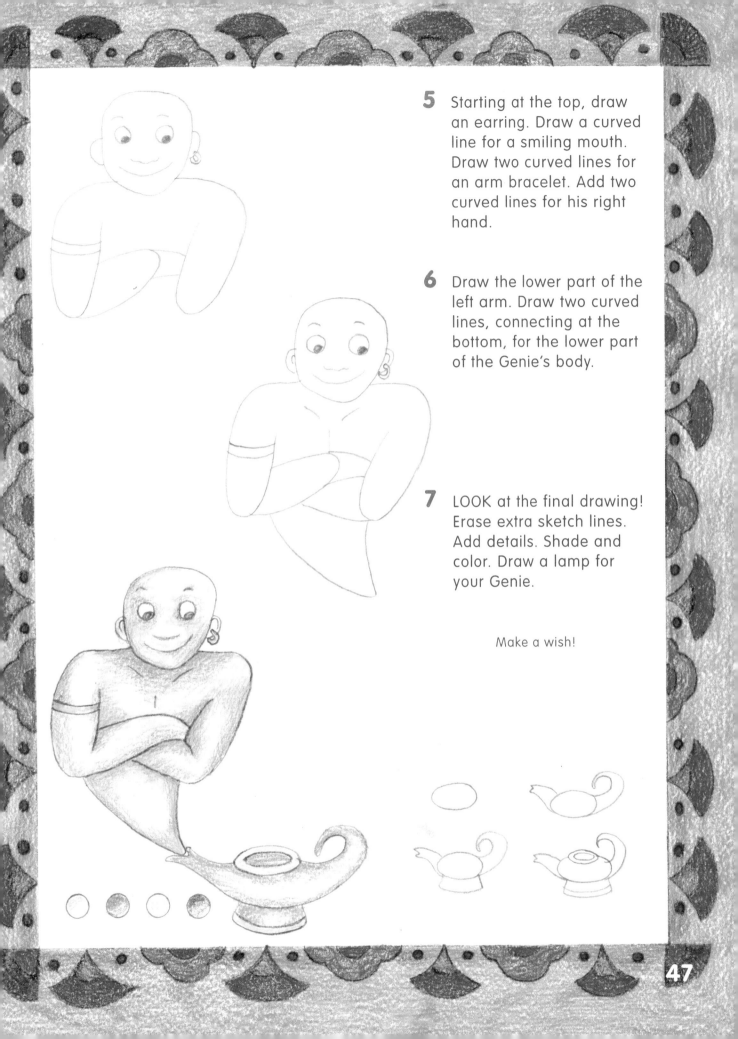

5 Starting at the top, draw an earring. Draw a curved line for a smiling mouth. Draw two curved lines for an arm bracelet. Add two curved lines for his right hand.

6 Draw the lower part of the left arm. Draw two curved lines, connecting at the bottom, for the lower part of the Genie's body.

7 LOOK at the final drawing! Erase extra sketch lines. Add details. Shade and color. Draw a lamp for your Genie.

Make a wish!

Fairy

Fairies are the most famous creatures of all folklore. They are tiny and can become visible or invisible at will. They are usually helpful but can also be tricksters. They love dancing and dainty food. To please a fairy, leave out a small dish of milk.

1   Sketch an egg for the head and a small rectangle for the upper body. Notice the position of the head.

2   Draw the eyes, nose and mouth, slightly to one side, as shown. Draw a curved line for the ear. Sketch a long oval shape to begin one upper arm.

3   Draw a curved line to begin the upper part of the other arm. Draw a curved line for the lower part of the first arm. Sketch a long oval shape to begin the top of one leg.

4   Draw a long curved line to begin the second leg. Sketch a small trapezoid to begin a hand. Sketch a long oval shape for the lower part of the first leg.

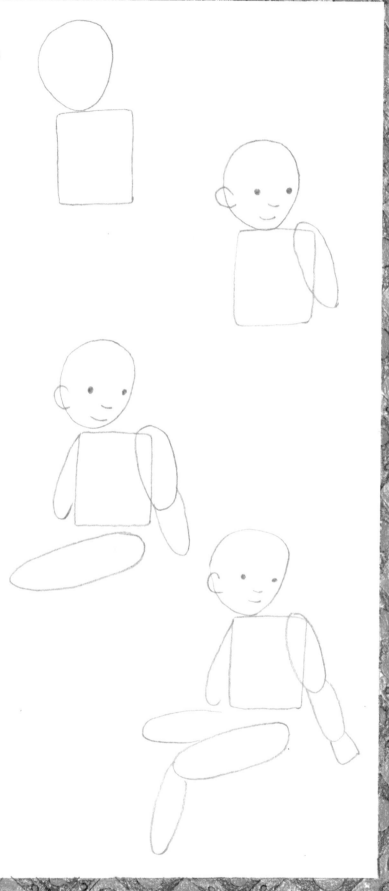

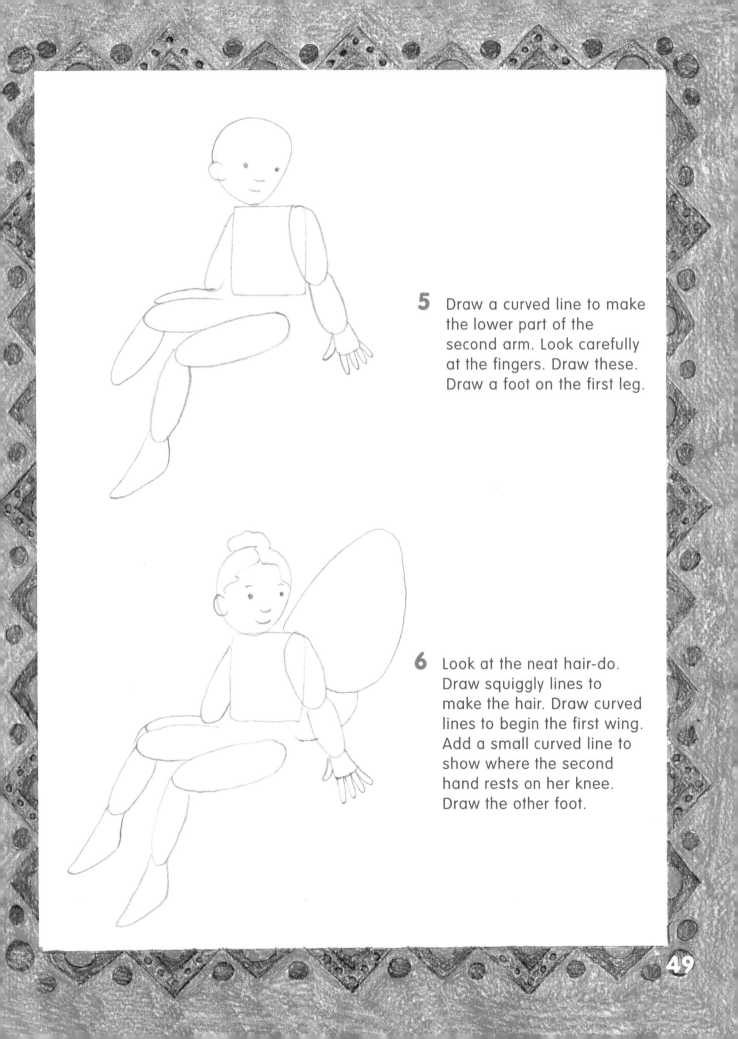

5 Draw a curved line to make the lower part of the second arm. Look carefully at the fingers. Draw these. Draw a foot on the first leg.

6 Look at the neat hair-do. Draw squiggly lines to make the hair. Draw curved lines to begin the first wing. Add a small curved line to show where the second hand rests on her knee. Draw the other foot.

7 Starting at the top, draw the second wing. Using curved lines, draw her dress neckline, sleeves and skirt.

8 LOOK at the final drawing! Erase extra guide lines. Add the details you see. Shade and color.

NOTE: Having the fairy sit on a leaf makes her look small. In Art, this is called changing SCALE. Try making big things small and small things big. EXPERIMENT!

Fabulous Fairy!

Troll

Trolls are unpleasant creatures that live in caves in Northern Europe. They are generally considered to be large, nasty, ugly, and dumb creatures who would, by the way, be very happy to eat you up. I'll bet they don't smell nice either.

1 Sketch a circle overlapping a square.

2 Erase the line across the circle. Look at that grumpy face. Draw the eyes, nose and mouth.

3 Using squiggly lines, draw two big hairy ears. Draw the eyebrows. Notice how it changes the Troll's expression. Draw a curved line on each side of the nose for nostrils.

4 Look at the shape of his beanie cap. Using curved lines, draw it. Add a small curved line inside each ear. Draw long lines to make his arms.

5 Draw jagged lines to make his shaggy beard. Add his raggedy pants.

6 Erase extra sketch lines. Look at the shape of his hands. Draw these. Draw the lower part of each leg.

7 Add a few fingers to his right hand. Using curved lines, draw his big feet. Give him a big, knobby club to lean on.

8 LOOK at the final drawing! Add the details you see. Shade and color.

Terrific Troll!

Brownie

Always helpful, the little Brownie is a household spirit of Scotland and England. They are happy to do chores and never ask for payment. In fact, a Brownie would consider payment insulting. To thank a Brownie, just leave some milk and a little cake where they will be likely to find it.

1 Sketch a tilted egg for the Brownie's head. Sketch a tilted square and trapezoid for the body.

2 Add two eyes, a nose, and a mouth. Draw two neck lines. Draw curved lines to make the upper part of the arms and the upper part of both legs.

3 Add little sticking out ears. Draw the lower part of both arms. Draw the lower part of both legs.

4 Look at the shape of each hand. Draw the hands and fingers. Look at the shape of the boots. Draw the boots.

5 Look at the hat. Draw it. Give him a broom handle to hold.

6 Look at the shape of his tunic. Draw the jagged lines to make the edges raggedy. Draw lines to make the bottom of the broom.

7 LOOK at the final drawing! Erase extra sketch lines. Add details. Shade and color.

Elf

Caretakers of the natural world, elves are the loveliest creatures that live in the land called Faerie. Although fond of playing tricks on humans, they are generally friendly and peaceful forest dwellers. They love music and magic.

1 Sketch an egg for the head and a square for the body.

2 Draw two eyes. Draw two curved lines for the neck. Sketch an overlapping oval for the upper part of one arm.

3 Add a nose and mouth. Sketch a curved line for the lower part of the first arm.

4 Draw flowers on your Elf's head. Add an ear. Draw a curved line to begin one hand. Draw a curved line to begin the other arm.

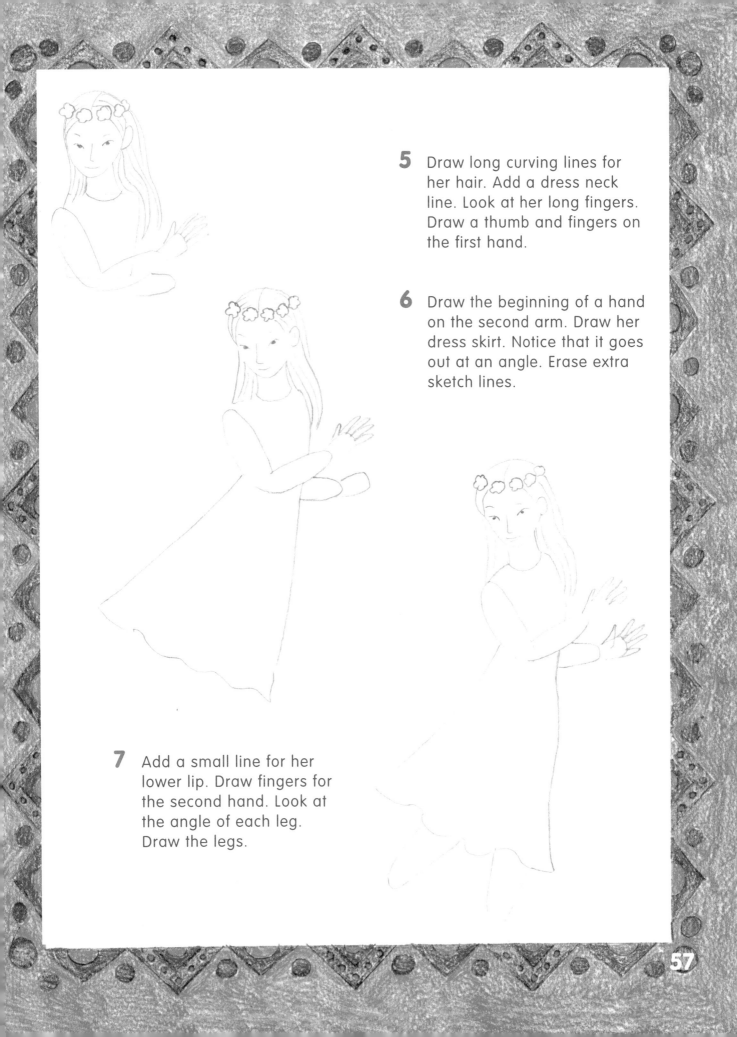

5 Draw long curving lines for her hair. Add a dress neck line. Look at her long fingers. Draw a thumb and fingers on the first hand.

6 Draw the beginning of a hand on the second arm. Draw her dress skirt. Notice that it goes out at an angle. Erase extra sketch lines.

7 Add a small line for her lower lip. Draw fingers for the second hand. Look at the angle of each leg. Draw the legs.

8 Starting at the top, draw a
circle inside each flower.
Look carefully at the dress.
Add the details you see.
Draw the feet.

9 LOOK at the final drawing!
Erase extra sketch lines.
Shade and color.

Excellent Elf!

Pixie

An English fairy the size of your hand, a pixie has squinty eyes, an upturned nose, and red hair. They often wear a green clothing and pointed caps. They help the poor and guide travelers at night. Pixies can be both helpful or tricky, so don't insult them or they will be sure to get even.

1 Sketch a tilted egg for the head. Sketch a tilted rectangle for the body.

2 Draw two eyes and an upturned nose. Draw a long curved line on each side for the arms.

3 Draw a mouth. Add a curved line to begin each hand. Draw long curved lines for the legs.

4 Add curved eyebrows. Draw ears. Look at the hands. Draw a thumb and fingers on each hand. Draw the feet.

5 Starting at the top, draw curls and a pointed cap for your Pixie. Add some round buttons to his jacket. Draw two long lines, held by his right hand, to begin the stem of a flower.

6 Look at the shape of the flower. Draw the flower and add two leaves to the stem. Draw a neckline on his jacket.

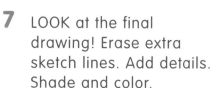

7 LOOK at the final drawing! Erase extra sketch lines. Add details. Shade and color.

NOTE: Making the flower big, makes the Pixie look small. Remember SCALE? When you change the SCALE in a drawing, you can make big things small and little things big. EXPERIMENT!

Leprechaun (LEP - ra - kon)

The story of Leprechauns comes from the folklore of Ireland. Leprechauns are clever little shoemakers who wear leather aprons, tall caps, and shoes with silver buckles. They are hard to spot and even harder to catch. If you do ever catch one, he is obliged to give you his pot of gold which he keeps at the end of the rainbow.

1 Sketch a tilted egg on top of a tilted trapezoid.

2 Draw two eyes, a nose, and a mouth. Draw a curved line to begin the upper arm.

3 Add a curved line for the lower part of the arm. Look at the angle of the leg. Draw it.

4 Add two ears. Draw a line to begin the hand. Draw the second leg.

5 Draw jagged lines for the Leprechaun's shaggy beard. Draw lines for the handle of the hammer in his hand. Look at the shape of his feet. Draw the feet.

6 Add the head of the hammer. Draw buckles on his shoes.

7 Draw lines to begin his hat. Draw his cobbler's bench.

8 Starting at the top, draw lines to finish the hat brim, band and buckle. Add a curved line for the other arm. Look carefully at the shape of the shoe he's repairing. Draw the shoe on the bench.

9 LOOK at the final drawing! Erase extra sketch lines. Add details. Shade and color. Give him a pot of gold and a rainbow!

Lucky Leprechaun!

Index

Drawing mythical creatures IS FUN.

This Rainbow-tongued Chaigabulion (KA-EE-GA-BOO-lee-un) by
Daniel Levin is part Chameleon, part Iguana, part bunny, and part lion!

Create a mythical creature of your own!

Learn about other
drawing books online at
www.drawbooks.com